YOU

~

HAGIOS
PRESS

YOU

~

Gary Hyland

HAGIOS PRESS
Box 33024 Cathedral PO
Regina, Saskatchewan S4T 7X2
www.hagiospress.com

Library and Archives Canada Cataloguing in Publication

Hyland, Gary, 1940-
You / Gary Hyland.

Poems.
ISBN 978-0-9783440-6-1

I. Title.
PS8565.Y53Y69 2008 C811'.54 C2008-905355-9

Edited by Paul Wilson.
Designed and typeset by Donald Ward.
Cover art: *Individualist*, by Lynn Huntly-Wyczolkowski, cibachrome, courtesy the Herringer Kiss Gallery, Calgary
Cover design by Yves Noblet.
Set in ITC Galliard.
Printed and bound in Canada.

The publishers gratefully acknowledge the assistance of the Saskatchewan Arts Board, The Canada Council for the Arts, and the Cultural Industries Development Fund (Saskatchewan Department of Culture, Youth & Recreation) in the production of this book.

for Sharon Nichvalodoff

Contents

~

YOU UNDERSTAND

NOT YOU

I LOVE(D) YOU

THE ABSENT AS IF PRESENT

This "You" Business

You needn't read this preface to enjoy the poems that follow. Indeed, you might find it dull or a hindrance. Should you discover yourself thinking that, O vocative one, please desist and move on to the main course.

One of the charges made against contemporary poetry is that it has grown increasingly obscure. That is a contentious issue, especially if one examines the research that reveals a decline of reading skills in the general population. On the other hand, one could counter that conclusion with the fact that the earlier data to which recent reading scores are compared was gathered when schools were more élitist. Then there is the whole question of the treatment of contemporary poetry in the classroom. And so on.

When one approaches the question from an examination of prosody and asks, "Are the practices of contemporary poets contributing to an alienation of would-be readers?" I think a qualified affirmative argument can be made. If we greatly narrow the subject to the use of pronouns, we can find some baffling practices.

"To hell with antecedents" seems to be the motto of some poets. A poem may begin with an unspecified "he," "she," "we," or "you." Of course, this can be a matter of *in media res,* cleared up by a later reference or inferences from context. But not always. Too often, the reader is left to try a number of possible scenarios, none of which seems to apply exactly.

If we narrow our considerations further to the ways poets employ the pronoun *you*, we can get more explicit. I recently did a survey of several newly published books of poetry, including one of my own, focusing on the usage of this word. Generally, the poets employed the pronoun in one of six modes.

First, there's the vocative *you*, used as subject or object, adopted when one or more persons is being addressed directly and always to be interpreted by the reader as though he or she is being spoken to, as in "The answer, perceptive reader, is no mystery to you."

The evocative *you* is a real or fictional person or persons, who is neither the writer nor the reader, being spoken of by a real or fictional person. In employing this mode, the writer is often adopting a persona. An example might be taken from *Hamlet:* "Mother, you have my father much offended."

The illustrative *you* is used in an abstract way to mean people in general, usually a substitute for the third-person singular *one* or *a person* and often in the imperative voice: "When grappling with the id, remember what you did."

The transmorphic *you* is often a substitute for the first-person pronoun *I*, after a text or speech has begun in the first person. This form is frequently used in informal speech when the speaker, consciously or unconsciously, wants to distance himself or herself from the occasion. For example: "Having told too many lies, I was cornered. In the end, you can't think of an honest way out."

The apostrophic *you* refers to one or more persons, objects, or abstractions who are absent but addressed as if present. A classic example would be Wordsworth's sonnet, "London 1801," which begins, "Milton! Thou shouldst be living at this hour."

Finally, there's the deliberately indeterminant *you*. The reader can never be sure of the antecedent of this pronoun, but that is inconsequential to understanding the poem. In fact, the writer may be creating ambiguity to amplify the meaning. Examples of these rare usages depend so much on context that they require quoting an entire poem, which I will forego.

Almost automatically, the poetry of love evokes the word *you*, and usually it is the evocative *you*. The person referred to may be regarded as sacred or reviled, desired or abhorred; the poet may be exultant or disappointed, depending on what stage of love's manifest illusions and rewards is being portrayed.

In the volumes I read, most readers would have little difficulty recognizing the poet's application of *you*, though there were some blurred cases. I have, though, found more imprecision in some literary journals.

The poems that follow explore relationships and variations on relationships with diverse people in these modes. Sometimes one mode is deployed for an entire section; other times, not. The poems were written long before they were organized this way and hardly ever without thought of employing this or that mode. Because the relationship of poet to reader fascinates me, there are poems, some of them saucy, where the *you* is you, the reader. There are playful poems in which the *you* is intentionally not identified, that say, "Try this on for size."

There are poems where the *you* is quite obviously me, the writer, attempting to share an experience. In other poems I am not me but have assumed another's identity. In some of these it is unimportant precisely who the *you* is. In one, I have the audacity to write as if I were a renowned American poet, and in some I speak as if I were well-acquainted with several others. As Sylvia Plath has said, "The worst enemy to creativity is self-doubt." I also speak to myself. In some poems, I am speaking to me as if I were a close friend; in others, a remonstrating parent. In no poems do I acquiesce to an appeal to loan money to myself.

There are those who claim the self is so all-encompassing and so dominant that we are prisoners in a perpetual state of subjectivity. "You are . . ." Who can resist not knowing the completion of that thought when it is spoken to you?

Most imaginative writing seeks to subvert that self-centred state, at least temporarily. It attempts to open vistas, shed a different light on old ones, or, by reflecting on the self, grope toward some sort of self-illumination. I hope that at least some of these poems do some of these things for you.

Gary Hyland
Summer 2008

You Are Here

~

YOU, YOU, YOU OR YOU?

Has it come to this, you
reading something you think you
could have scribbled on a bus, jostled
by people with briefcases, bags, earphones
full of peculiar music, you
waiting to discover how you
relate to it, who you are now, who
this *you* is?

            Is it the *you*
know you a bodiless
everyone?
            Or the transmorphic
you who begins as I?

Or a fragment of a fragmented writer
addressing another fragment, perhaps
mind to body, thus: *Must you,*
overfamiliar, dense companion,
be there always?
                        Or another you –
not-you, a stand-in, the writer's
lover perhaps, with you
a voyeur at their window?

Has it come to this
tumble of conjectures,
you left guessing
which you might be you,
while slowly your life seeps
under the door?

EXASPERATING, IRRITATING, INFURIATING, AGITATING

Think of this as the only sentence on this page,
dawdling along the predetermined streets of written
discourse, which reflect our propensity for gridiron
alignments as in our cities and our lives, its left-right
destination, at this stage, uncertain, equally fogged its
meaning and relevance, thus exasperating the impatient
and practical, not to mention those who require a
payload of moral or spiritual glitter or at least gilt
tidbits of style with witty croutons, or an unexpected
fracturing of the rectangular, perhaps a trendy crescent
here, there a serpentine departure, later some open
white breathing space that plays against the linearity
the eye, by convention, expects, itself not unlike that
at which Blake railed in his native city's streets and
psyche, and by opposition to soldierly progression,
in the name of radical art, makes a statement so
profound it transmogrifies the soul and yet does not
frustrate those plagued with ego who fail to recognize
themselves in the window ghosts along the way and
who, in their often jaded haste and self-obsession, are
irritated by even the most unobscured challenge (such
as Blake, such as his city, also, less evidently, Alan Jay
Lerner) nor do they locate solace in this languid shape
and pace that also infuriates the primly pure and their
naive kin who have long since concluded by form, by
sound, by custom, by Frost-this ain't no poem, but
we can assume those most afflicted thus have much
sooner disembarked agitated at what is evidently, to
them, an effusion of undifferentiated crud, leaving the
long-suffering editor and the self-indulgent author
together with the object of this ramble and gem of
their admiration-heroic and indomitable
you.

IS THIS ABOUT YOU?

If your right foot is in a cast
because you kicked your neighbour's cat
in winter and lo and behold
it was already dead and frozen,
this poem is not about you.

If you are the spouse of a banker,
this poem is not about you.

If you have attempted or
thought seriously about
repairing a defective condom,
this poem is not about you.

If you are inclined to wonder
what animals you encounter
on a random basis (say gophers
by the roadside) are thinking,
this poem is not about you.

If you spend days coring apples
to create organic art objects,
this poem is not about you.

Never worn a hand-me-down?
Never kicked an empty can?
This poem is not about you.

If at this moment you could be
making love with a lover
you have not made love with
for over two weeks, but you
would prefer not to,
this poem is not about you.

If you have never had an orgasm
when no one else was present,
this poem is not about you.

If you believe the phrase
the spouse of a banker
contains a sexist assumption,
this poem is not about you.

If in the last month
you have danced with someone
other than yourself,
this poem is not about you.

If you have never postponed
bathing because no one
was likely to notice,
this poem is not about you.

If you consider these exclusions
disrespectful or derogatory,
stop reading this poem.
It is not about you.

If you think it should be about you
this poem is not about you.

If this poem is not about you
or me (banished early)
or all those worthy others,
then who is it about?

THIS POEM IS ABOUT YOU

What does this have to do with
you   A consideration
        to corrupt any proposition

As if you exist
anywhere but in the nostril
of your mind
As if language were God's finger
articulated to pick
                                        your condition
As if those humans contriving
        not to be killed by
one foe or another
                                three billion or so
should harvest beans
for your chocolate dreams

Not that you have a choice
You are indelibly   you

Gorged on your high-calorie
limitations and imperfections
the monster who squats
on you   with its
moon-sized ass
isn't about to
depart for better rumping
        in the nose-pit galaxy
of some other life form

Smile
This is
all
there is

and it's
        you

THE POEM OF THE ACT OF THE MIND

> Where the wild poem is a substitute
> For the woman one loves or ought to love.
> Wallace Stevens
> "Arrival at the Waldorf"

Wallace Stevens writing at the Waldorf
on embossed and crested letterhead
in dense stanzas his theory of verse.

Before love, to end quarrels, after
numbers make us winners or losers –
words, their matrix of exchanges.

You, twice removed, reading this, saying
what you are saying to yourself –
the ways language complicates.

Without you, nothing. That's love.
Or tennis. One here. One there. Phantom
volleys coursing between. Turn on turn.

Let's erase the boundary lines. If we each
score love while playing well, we'll win.

ANOTHER POEM ABOUT YOU

Is this poem about you in the sense
everything you encounter is about you?

Does it know the deeper secrets
of your inner cravings,
your doomed passions?

Will it cozy up, try to be your friend
luring you to reveal what
you had planned to forever conceal?

Does it think you represent humanity?
Will it allude to you as a Jungian pixel
on the screen of the vast collective unconscious?

None of the above.

It is about you and like you will always be
finite and aching to be so much more.

HERE

Never mind if we exist
mind and body as we think or
as figments and fragments.
That which we are frets
that we are not enough
or misunderstood or
unloved when we should be
delighted just to be
such as we are.

When darkness
snouts our windows,
that I can say *this*
and you can read *this*
with the variations
you assume or cannot avoid
is sufficient cause
for celebration.

We are not Atlantic or Pacific
but both and all the stops between
the oceans of stars
and the orbiting dust
of the dead.

It is I but not me, you
but not you, who come
as close to love as love
allows in this place before
final revisions.

SOLARITY

Always you have been at the centre
too brilliant to be seen.

What can that mean? Can it be about you
the way the universe is?

Of course. Of course not. The observer's
dilemma. Even praise misses you.

If only we knew, each in orbit, ablaze.
You are more than a deluge of light

with blemishes, more than instruments
can record. Your emissions disrupt

communications, all of which are about
you, even when they aren't.

That language of exquisite characters
beautiful beyond translation

and without meaning to us –
you are that language.

Observer. Observed. Light. Darkness.
You.

COVENANT

What you think about winter,
its skitterings of snow over
frozen plains, how we live
on the blade-ends of truth
in fields deep in white deceit,
I don't know. I don't know you.

You are somewhere in a room
I have never entered, until now.
It is the way of our covenant
for me to abide in your presence
and let you grant such space
today as we can both create.

We are like players who stay
a long time at the game, while
elsewhere in the building, fire
nibbles in the furtive way of
vague dangers everywhere,
the better to engulf us.

Meanwhile we waver in patience –
with each other, with the game,
with the losses we must
endure to make such small gains,
these blades we devour, grateful
they survive the wide and perilous plains.

SALVATION

This poem's as boring as leaves wet with rot.
Not the rush of a dagger to your throat.
(Can it be too long before you crave
a larger, colder blade, a shave,
a slit near your carotid?)

No sudden shit on the classroom floors
stoking consternation. (Such lore's
hardly new to a cool school kid.)
Severed heads won't hiss

blood in your face. Should you yawn this
doesn't spit novelty. (Not much
noticed in the rain of sludge.)

No alarms to panic the docile citizen.
(Unglancing in the sterile din.)

Rescue this. (And yourself.)

I KNEW IT WOULD BE YOU

I knew it would be you first glance so you're not
fooling me sitting there looking calm but wanting
your reptilian brain stroked not to mention
a consequential buzz in your frontal lobe
as if at last after all those pages of blah
blah & blah finally what you really want
hits you between the wherever you'd like
& you may be thinking it's annoying to be
thus addressed here but if your expectations
are not met at least up to now
consider they may be unrealistic or that
you are jaded having read a few thousand
too many efforts like this forming bad habits that
several lines previous caused you to miss
a trope so subtle this whole rib-lined scrag
of a pestering poem became super cosmic
& fireworked inside perceptive minds which
you may still possess having fallen into the
stupor unpunctuated jabber seems to produce
for which this poem accepts complete responsibility
although the truth is it hardly cares you're there
is content to hunker a streak on a sheet
hardly ever regarded & then hastily
by someone wanting a personal revelation
now if you don't mind at a time when just
getting to the bottom of the page is all the poem
can manage to imagine the poet bogged with
personal adversities which he sublimates
in creative chaos subsequently inflicted
on you as art   hah & yes he has slipped
on the reportorial 3rd person kimono
likely to deflect fault which it seems he has
more than a damn lot of trouble with
to the extent it makes him hypersensitive
& that explains how I knew it would be you

MEADOWLARK

You sing note-perfectly of being
here on the grasslands in the sun under
the brilliant sky. On your lichened boulder
you all but burst with the bliss of seeing
the land outflow your eye over wheat fields
brimming green. Even the shadow of a hawk
gliding past does not cause you to break
from the ecstasy your gazing yields.
The light drives you into song and us who
listen into silence and surprise
that we are between two versions of blue
with variations beyond our ears and eyes.
Warfare, pain, pandemics, poverty?
Sky, you sing, with intricate simplicity.

THE BOOK THAT KNOWS IT'S A BOOK

1.

Smart-ass thing butts its rump into my life. Cheeky as the back side of a truck full of porkers, it doesn't care, stands on hind hooves, demands how many anal references I've detected thus far. *Read me,* it demands like a talent show candidate so eager to have mediocrity transformed to fame he stands on the restaurant table (one foot sliding in someone's Caesar) and performs impromptu for the sponsors, three women dressed as four men in suits smoking small cigars and drinking Southern Comforts.

Whatever I was reading didn't count one sparrow's fart. This tome, its cover garish as the Las Vegas strip with a hard-on, wants between the lobes of my mind to hump out its dribble of micro-squirmy intentions.

2.

The book plunges in defecating obscurities and trifles enough to fertilize the Gobi, grabbing the sleeve of my very best go-to-meeting sweater and pulling it out of shape so that it hangs on my forearm like the coleonic cavity of some giant annelid forerunner of the mucousy Lumbrici that rained up from the garden every so-so summer of my so-so youth.

I want to get read, it secretes with all the throaty innuendo of a laryngitis-plagued hooker, its elongated cilia tickling my nostrils, the air sick with the fumes of its secretions. *You'd better be good,* I say. *Oh, I am, I am,* it purrs. *I'll be whatever you read. Read me loose, baby, read me to the end of rhyme.* And so it began.

3.

It has the subtle rumble of a gale bawdy-checking your walls and windows, not to mention a forest on the edge of things at dusk casting murkiness between sensibility and intellect subtly apparent in that allusions to arcana are profoundly superficial, in spite of ample justification that normal discourse is inadequate for expressing the sensual, mystical, and numinous, as manifest in lines about a salmon snared in the speaker's aortic valve or Charon on the Saskatchewan, word warpings with Latin limbs fused to Greek torsos.

4.

Look, it says, *look here, don't look there,* in a thin wattage of visionless seeing, my eyes red from its blast of syllables, mind fuzzed from the ambush of savage associations and metaphysical couplings. Inside its costumes you find . . . costumes. They sparkle with shards of selfhood, shreds of shabby universals, small oval mirrors inset so that the reader can see himself reading while the book whispers, *You, you, you,* meaning you.

YOU ARE HERE

in a room holding something made of paper
impressed with ink.

I am there in a room trying to concentrate words
that will make you think

we are brilliant, beautiful, amazing or at least
not a stain on the planet,

not ornate or slick words such as you might see
chipped into public granite

or spangled on a greeting card, or kept,
folded like a precious text

or necessary code secreted in your wallet
for whenever next

you need it. So here's the two of us now,
me and you, hurtling through space

and time. Of course, my now is prior
to yours. I may, in any case,

given my condition, be dead. Regardless,
you and this contrivance

have met, made contact, almost touched
and that is not by chance.

You Know

~

FUTURE STREET

Someone walks toward you pushing
the future like a baby carriage. You believe
this person will know you and where you are
among the throngs on the street. You think
it desirable to approach the future looking
ahead as far as you can. You think you see it.

Two people stop to talk, a man and woman,
and you almost crash into them, into their lives.
It would have changed everything,
you intruding, apologizing at that moment.
For them. For you, errant in their equation.

This on a bright day with pressing errands
and by the curb a sack of commitments
you dumped. It knows where you live,
will be on the step when you get home.

A gunman could run from that bank,
his reflection still rotating in the door,
and knock you to the pavement. In fact,
he does. You notice his cowboy boots,
the reek of smoke. He pushes down on you
to hoist himself up, briefcase in one hand,
gun in the other. A voice barks at him
to halt as he leaps into a van that speeds off.

While people gather, a woman helps you up.
It is the woman who was talking.
As she bends over you her hair falls forward
and the fragrance pulls like a leash. You rise
easily upward in the river of her eyes.

In Ireland centuries ago
someone threw bones and stones
on a red velvet cloth and there you were
on this street, squinting under the canopy
of your hand past blocks of traffic
and then whacked to the sidewalk
by a reckless man. And then this woman
and her companion. It was a baffle then.
If it has never happened yet, it will.

ON JUDGING A POETRY CONTEST

Back when choosing was easy
you chose to be the one who chooses.

Stacks of words wanting validation,
the chance to flash their craft, brash or subtle.

Twelve dozen supplicants craving
the skyward lift in one of eight modes –

1. Flinch while I jab this blade into
   my pain. My bleeding is your bleeding.

2. I will undulate on dactyls, dance
   to the gusts of the westerly wind.

3. With string theory and Vedic theology
   I will reveal the nonexistence of your soul.

4. I wear jeans, speak straight, my hand on
   yours. There's skill enough in that.

5. See how this and this are placed near
   this with an impressive imported twist?

6. I will tell you the secrets of lilacs, how
   they compose in palest mauve.

7. Look what I do with dust and memories,
   how my handmade lines fret their frames.

8. I am the one that holds all of these.
   That shapes their chaos into harmonies.

In time you make three choices. In time,
vowing this is the last time, you raise one high.

THE POET AS PARANOID STEWARD

In your closet, your shirts snarl about
pressing civil rights by which they mean
they have not properly been ironed.
The blue flannel is the instigator
claiming violations of cuffs
trailed through ice cream and gravy.
The others mumble – wash water too hot,
armpit pong, over-crowded conditions,
sweaty collar grime, pens secreting,
buttons hanging by a thread,
colour-negating forced integration
of mixed washing. They plot reprisals –
deviant sleeves, tangles and wrinkles,
twisted collar tips, loose button holes.
The sweaters start to whisper yarns.

The food in your cupboards is restless.
He shuns fibre the bran flakes growl
Beta carotene sniff the apricots
and the litany swells: peanut butter
charging niacin privation, sardines
alleging deficient vitamin D,
molasses citing inadequate iron.
They make plans to picket your stove.

Your computer claims neglect is abuse
and is plotting a massive purge.

Come home from the bar at your peril.

MORE THAN THE WORDS

You must love me more than the words you use
to love me, leaving me for them at night
and mornings. Times you are with me and gone
into the darkness where you grope for them.
I've heard you rave about a crow or how
some light slipped a blind to transform a room.

Write no contracts or treaties. Never vow
eternal anything without your
calculator.
                    Yes, I know you love me.
Your words don't make it so is all I say,
as sweet and fine and heartfelt as they are.
And I love you, though my saying it
is just a whisper in this turbulence,
good just so far as I am good to you.

NO POEM

A thunk, a surge of muffled sobs,
mother crumpled on the floor,
father hulking over her, me
white-knuckled to the headboard.

And some constipated academic wimp
in his cushy office with his zippy
new computer writes all this
into a poem – a po-em, for fucksakes.

He takes a pack of dainty words,
tarts them up with sprinklies
and confettis them on a page
for all the other little pinky people

to do those wispy things they do
when they think they're into
whatever they think life is
after they've turned it milky

safe and oh so nice.
                                        No poem
ever grabs your arm and whacks
you with a razor strap till you've got
white welts on your red welts.

No pretty bunch of words stops your
shrieking or gets into your guts
good enough so you don't become
your mother and your father.

DAY WITH BOUTS OF FROST

All day the day has spoken to me.

Lines like that call for specification.
Don't dump on the reader more of that glum
Flutter a shotgun couldn't blast meaning from.

None of that public semaphore by cloud,
Nor anything to chirp iambically.

What an outright cowardly evasion
And stumble stone, a poem about being
A poem and one too obvious at that,
Plus you are *doing the two-step routine*
Though rhyme and cadence have both gone flat.

More as if someone had pulled me from a crowd
And taken me aside for a special declaration,
An honour of which I might have been proud
Had I understood the situation.

If you want a poem to sing don't force it
To be anything but what it wants to be
In words that don't boggle, lines that don't jerk.

But what the day whispered in its plain voice
Was its light had been entering my eyes
For too many years and I would never see
its miracles because I had made the choice
to plod, and it should come as no surprise
therefore that God could not share the light with me.

You've got this one twisted in a corset
too trite for sense. Let it die for mercy
And find yourself some honest line of work.

ONE OF THE INFINITE WAYS

The perfect poem is
what it says
a compulsion
you complete
and incorporate

Its half-brother
also craves life
in your life
even though it has
failed in one
of the infinite ways

The one for instance
that talks flatly of itself
after the one it wanted to be
was strangled mid-dance
by a scarf
of allusions

It quavers
on its thin stem
dreaming of

perfection
the trophy
of your eyes
your voice saying
I love you

TOO GLIB, TOO SLICK, TOO CUTE AND QUICK

Your poems are a little too finished,
you say. I think you mean they're all gloss
and gleam without the smudge of fingerprints.

There's so much symmetry, you explain,
pleased I'm not contending or in a mope,
all these tidy forms and stanza structures.

And, frankly, your endings are much too pat,
you add, *and there's a slickness that suggests*
glibness, a hocus-pocus of showy effects.

I tell you of my friend the painter who left
some of his canvasses incomplete to show
he knew his problem was completion.

That's it, you say. *Exactly what I mean.*
Just rough cut a poem and –

REJECTION NOTE

Listen, attractive as you are, you are
unattractive with that reed jammed in your face,
your lips groping, desperate, your cheeks bloated
then collapsing into ghostly hollows.
You think you have the goods. You have the heart,
but you haven't got the heat. You ember
occasional never-before phrases, but
you're so inside the box it's a coffin.
Too easy that way, though you may grunt
and sweat digging up all those well-used graves.
In fact, your work echoes an old wiz, played
these parts back in the earlies, a cheeky Greek
named Marsyas. You could check him out,
though I doubt you will. Or maybe you have.

MEMORY TRICK

> One night a poem grows in him
> like a tree it grows in the dark
> he awakes impaled on its trunk
>
> Anne Szumigalski
> "Quince"

Last night was your last invasion, you thugs.
How many years have I lost to your divine
attacks? Sleep, love and leisure wiped by your drugs?
Abducted and confined inside your lines.
Insinuators. Seducers. Swindlers. Thieves.
Whatever your crimes I have served the time.
I've studied like the victim of a disease
your beguiling spiels, your lures, your wiles.
I know what aspirations, what vanities
mingle with your easy ecstasies.
I have mastered the nays of mockingbirds,
the coy repulsion, the plush barricade.
I have alarms on my alarms. These words?
A software trick my memory played.

You Understand

FACE

The face at the window
late at night, that lunatic
alight with the grace of the moon,
holds in his dark-side brain
all you'll ever know
of anything, and one thing more.

While you pace the fallacy
of your house, chase illusions
beyond, it places its body
inside things as they are
from decaying leaf to poverty.
It knows how not to be itself.

Nothing of your conception
is as it is. The mind with your
face will never know this
the way the madman does.
In yet another deception
you call this your reflection.

IMPERFECTION

– Weyburn, Saskatchewan, 1957

The mind tries to draw itself and fails,
the eye gazing into a disturbed pond,
the hand sketching crude circuitry.

You and all that's not you add up
to everything.
                        But the spirit of you
that will be gone from life when you are gone,
soul, or psyche, essence or gnostic spark
is a wisp of mist in a distant sky.

Blood drips from the clotting gash in Christ's side
onto your brow as you look up at him
on the cross. It trickles into your eye.
LSD or reality? The brain knows
not. Nor cares. From now on you believe
the mind is a gift with which you love.

HUMANKIND

We've learned to prefer you over the others
with skin, bones, and scanty clothes,
the flies on their lips, their xylophonic ribs.
Your demands strike us less urgently
like the moon drawing up the oceans.
Your injuries leave us unsplattered.
You starve without stench, waste without decay.
We can fund the right institutions
to house and nourish you in our names
and send you love with the click of a mouse.
Thank you for leaving our doors unknocked,
our phones unwrung, our monitors for games.
You ache with such distance and dignity
we hail your incorporeality.

DEMONS OF THE VOID: A – B = 0

> [In deriving equation 5] we have divided by zero and we get the ridiculous statement that 1 = 0. From there we can prove any statement in the universe, whether it is true or false.
>
> Charles Seife
> *Zero: The Biography of a Dangerous Idea*

When you peer in the oval mirror of
zero, do you see a nonexistent rascal

or the mouth to a crimped digestive
tract? *There's nothing to fear,* said Pascal,

but in Saskatchewan you are restive
with space and when the beast roars you pulse

as its demon breath halos your head.

Permit
a set of equations with the premise

each of a and b is 1. Good. Later, let
both sides of equation 4 be divided by a

– b, and suddenly you become a blue-grey
Austrian songbird named Adolf Hitler.

This proof can be shown beyond palter
once Zero flexes its vast power to alter.

COLLISION

Just before it
hits the pane
the bird sees
a bird flying
into its eyes.

Its brain fills
with bone
concluding
the start of a reflex
of avoidance.

By the time you say
what was that
its body
is burning
a nest in the snow.

CALCULATING THE HORSE

> Some believe the end will come
> in the form of a mathematical equation.
> Others believe it will descend as a shining horse.
>
> Sarah Manguso
> "The Rider"

Of course death is an equation,
an igloo of water in a sea of ferns,
strange terms in mad presentation.
Who travels there? Who returns?

It also descends as a silver horse
to the plains, mountains, islands, seas,
out of sun onto us in swift course.
We mount and ride blind through these.

Saddle your equation. Jab a spur
into an exponent's side and
grasp the pommel fast and sure.
Soon you will sprawl on foreign land.

Enter the circular stable and see
how many horses make a king's pride.
(The Sumerians did and gave us 60.)
How many days can you stay astride?

With tables and instruments,
simplify and solve the complex,
calculate horse and path into sense.
In the end, the answer will be x.

EARLY SIGNS

> Forgetting, misplacing, repeating could be early signs of Alzheimer's.
>
> TV bulletin, Sept. 24, 2006

What was that? What did she say?
Something about pearly wines.
What about them? *Seems oldtimers*
make 'em. Mmmh, Where's the remote?
Not in the refrigerator.
The refrigerator? *Where you put it*
last week. Never did. I asked where
it is, not was. *Where what is?*
The geezly remote control. *Why?*
So I can change to the news channel.
We just watched the news. The other
news channel. *Why?* To see
if there's some newer news. Where is it?
What? What? *What're you looking for?*
I'm not looking for anything.
You were so. No, I wasn't. *Okay.*
Let's try us some of those pearly wines.

ONE LAST TIME

> Husband: The doctor says I will die before another daybreak. Let's have champagne and make love one last time.
> Wife: Easy for you – you don't have to get up in the morning.
>
> Joseph Brodsky, 1940-1996

That is not the way it will be – a prelude
of bubbly to a night of slow love-
making, though it beats having a nurse shove
a hypo in your arse while you exude
various waste products much the way
you did at first, except the clammy sweat
that comes of your heart's attempt to rally
for one more scramble from the valley
of the shadow where you tremble yet.
In time our making – of love, of scenes,
of poems – falls away like frosted leaves,
the season's prolonged divestment.
That you chortle at the prospect means
part of you still resists and grieves
the thinning light, the last diminishment.

THE WISDOM OF FOOD

Do not doubt your lunch knows
where it must go, what it must do.

Slice a carrot, hold a cross-section to your
eye and you will be eye to eye with an eye.
Eat and enhance blood flow to your eyes.

Press a tomato tenderly to your chest
It will sing a duet with your heart
about being four-chambered and red.
and grapes hang in heart-shaped clumps
the better to vitalize your blood.

Crack a walnut and behold the brain–
hemispheric, cerebrum and cerebellum,
complete with a wrinkly cortex and enough
neuro-transmitters to light your life.

Onions cleanse our dirty cells.
Kidney beans for kidneys.
Celery and rhubarb resemble bones
and to our bones they are a boon.

Sweet potatoes dart to their twins
the pancreas where they
teach the glycemic index
of diabetics what balance is.

Avocados and pears target womb
and cervix. How long to grow an avocado?
Nine months. No coincidence.
Olives are for ovaries
Citrus fruits for breasts.

Hanging in twosomes
crammed with seeds
figs are scrotal
to battle male sterility.

By their shapes shall you know them.
By their shapes they call out to you
to save your life with their deaths.

Never mind the banana.

OLD MAN WITH GUITAR

Your music in the noisy pub
curves from where large hands trouble
the nylon strings like sad guests.
You lean to the guitar, white hair

over your face, shoulders hunched.
Songs I hadn't heard, perhaps your own,
meditative, with now and then a slow
swirl of Spanish or Brazilian.

It reminds me of a maestro –
Django, Jobim, maybe Montoya?
I don't know – who said something like:
Music is full of spaces in which we make

notes. God creates silences into which
we place lovely noises. In the buzz
I feel the space around your notes.
I can see drops of sweat fall

through the light onto your guitar.
I hear the silences lengthening,
watch the hands waver and delay.
Then the music stops mid-phrase,

starts again and teeters into space.
For a long time you remain bent over
the instrument as if you were asleep
in the babble. Someone in the back

starts to clap, stops when people stare.
Then you look up. Your cheeks are wet.
You lean the guitar against the side of
the stool and shuffle off the stage.

The chattering continues. The waiter
breaks in with a drink I must have ordered.
Later, as I leave, it is still there,
the guitar, gleaming in a beam of light.

Not You

~

YOUR RAIN

You were nine the summer of the two-week rain.
A constant sunless drizzle which left grey puddles
in your brain that have never ebbed.

No television, no money for amusements,
yards and fields too soggy for play, you read
comics and invented games with bottle caps.

It came into you, that rain, came in and remained
in a way with no explaining, a dream that abides.
The scent of lilacs drenched, the lonely rooftop drone

became a soothing that unravels strain, expels it
with the soft pummel of the almost misty drops,
replaces it with a warm and tranquil room.

Your sleep was never more complete those days,
waking to the glisten of the window, the feeling
that being with yourself was all you needed.

Sometimes you come upon it and enter it again
and the tensions you beget recede – that child
safe in a long, long bliss with all the world at peace.

AFTER RAIN

The plop of the last raindrops off the roof
dropping into the wooden rain barrel
soothe him as he sits arched against it
on the wet ground, knees propping chin,

weeds reaching his knees and waving
in the breeze. He is thinking nothing
as he listens to the sound of the big drops
plopping and the surfing of the weeds.

From the lane you see only his head
above the weeds, seeming to ride them
like a wader in deep water. He looks neither
happy nor sad, seated against the barrel,

in the waving weeds, the neighbour boy,
chin on knees. Likely he clasps his ankles
or his shins. Likely he is daydreaming
of something to complete his small life.

His mother's face appears in the window
above the barrel. She would not see him
huddling nor read his thoughts any better
than you. On the porch she calls his name.

He hears his name breaking his not thinking
daze. He sees the neighbour gazing from
the lane. And then another plop. His mother
saying his name is not enough. He stays.

THE SKATE

Your memory goes to that morning, you trudged
to hockey practice, equipment bag hobo-style
on your stick over your shoulder, the sun too pale
in the cold eastern sky to make shadows.

You plodded beneath the Fourth Avenue Bridge,
over the CN tracks, sat on some cinders,
and, fogged in clouds of your breathing, laced
on your skates, tied the bag to your waist,

and skated slowly up the snow-free, wind-free
river, half a mile, lugging the canvas bag
behind, heading into the rising sun, now
a shade of yellow-pink you'd never seen,

With each recall you skate faster, the light
is larger, more surreal. Soon, only light.

SELF-PORTRAIT IN A DARK ROOM

1.

There is no mirror to break. No shard
to hold beneath your heart to make it speak.

By touch, by sound you try to spark
a memory of light. And fail

to produce a face. As if that matters.
As if your face is not a common illusion.

As if the surface is enough of anything,
and the eyes hold all we know of soul.

You often mistake yourself for someone
else. A veteran of an awful war.

Others have mistaken you for worse,
soldier boy, returning your own salute.

Everyone is wrong about everyone else,
all those secrets wasting in secret places.

2.

Nothing is apparent but a fear of nothing.
Which is death. Which is annihilation.

Why do you shake with inchoate desire
and make inexplicable explanations?

This very undertaking, these words
you strangle out as if your last?

Who places the garrote, makes
the bloodless constriction? Turn

and no one is there. And who would trade
time for trite stratagems, the play

of sounds echoing past contrivances?
You left the room before you entered.

Things like that. Or just a boy in the dark
gauging angry voices from the kitchen.

3.

You are absent from your self-portrait,
say you became the frame – a cliché.

How stale to imitate yourself to your-
self, to penetrate from exterior

gray matter to inner gray matter,
to always enter the room you left.

You want to stay where you are, rip
the floorboards and expose your

infected basement, the foundation
glazed with the faded paint of old desires.

With you reflected in his glasses,
the shrink says *Such a common conceit.*

How boring to be no one but yourself,
to be so unenigmatically – plain.

AS EVER

The air you draw into your lungs
departs soured with your
particular earthy odour

So much youness and all of it
grown so chronic
you thirst for a transmuting tonic

You've never once not been you
in sun, moon or incandescent light
and all the latitudes of night

Those exotic trips outside beyond
your self those wild scary
flights – all imaginary

So predictable you've become
to yourself you can foretell
when and how you'll rebel

You will not wake up a locust
not mutate through prayer
not look and not be there

Therefore
(risking the doctrinaire)
compose yourself with care

MY FATHER CALLED FOR WATER WHEN HE DIED

At fifteen, the movie Bedouins from
Romberg's *Desert Song* beguiled him.
Life had to be as sudden and entire
as the Riffs riding over the crest
of a dune, black cloaks cracking,
singing tunes with perfect words.

Water was my father's last word,
dying alone in the Sahara
he built as the set for his life.

Golf clubs slung from the saddle
of his camel, he would have saved
us from the Mahdi and Rommel
while we applauded like those first
movie audiences safe in an oasis
of chocolate, popcorn and kisses.

You drink a lot in the sand traps,
your heart shrivelling far from
the ports of recognition.
Your eyes squint against mirages
of mirages that would lure
you to boneyards. Nights you huddle
under a sky, mocked by stars
that shimmer large as glacial lakes.

In the end, straining to hear
a soundtrack promise of salvation,
hoof beats, drums, a desert boat,
he scanned the barren room for good
Arabs, for anyone who cared enough
to plod those last dunes with him.
There were none. Not even me. Just
the infinite sand clogging his throat.

THIS THEN

That you will die. That it will be soon.
Death's branch operation in your head
pumps invisible agents to swallow your days.

That no one cares much. Not even you.
That pills cannot restore you. Nothing
you do will change anything.

That up to the moment the door closes
you will drudge at inconsequential tasks
while your true devotions starve in cells.

Angels will not sing you to your rest.
What angels have you feathered? The angel
of self-interest? The wings of contrary affections?

Your angels tried but could not love you.
They sleep in the vestibule of grace,
sickly spirits, psoriatic, carbuncled.

That the white drifts on your wished-for slopes
are the bones of misshapen animals
that foraged on your meagre underbrush.

That you will stumble there like a pilot
downed, nose dribbling, mind driveling,
while the search teams stay home.

STILL LIFE ON THE BEACH

Today, we find ourselves on the sand,
shoeless, sockless, pants rolled to our knees.

Gulls circle so far at sea they look like flakes
of stray foam. We cannot hear their screeches.

We are alone. We do not know who may
have painted us or where the others have strayed.

Sure of what I will say, you say nothing.
Anticipating, I respond silently.

You are halfway right about me and wholly
wrong. And I read you as accurately.

We watch the ocean advance in long lines.
The breakers blur in the shallows, making

white aprons that undulate along the shore.
Their long and constant sighing means nothing.

FROM FAR OFF A CREED

We are never born, and we never die.
Paint that on your cheek with a tear for the myth
of death, those thousands you mourned in agony,
the pangs of longing to fill your lungs one more
day. In Ages past in Samarkand they
knew the sum of life on life, backward
and forward, was infinity.
When blood
seeps from your eyes, when the beast that feeds on
you bloats and shrieks along your nerves, when your
enemy's axe cleaves your spine, remember
the illusionist's spectacle is sanctioned
by the mighty to make you squirm and weep.
Will you clasp the ease of this alien creed
entire, here on the portal of your going?

TO SARAH WHO WROTE A LOVE POEM FOR A FRIEND

Can language make love? Why so many love-forsaken poets? Cravings fulfilled, love at last achieved, routine wilts desire. Eloquence sags. We love Rostand's Cyrano. But the real Cyrano would have pin-cushioned Christian and spirited Roxane away to live in diminishing bliss under the shadow of his nose. Nothing compels great passion like loneliness.

Occasionally, leave the pursuit of love. Create a cave in time, excluding the mundane, shunning obligations. Locate your mind in a favourite place. Escapism? Ah, but yes. The way being in Flatbush today you are not in Saskatchewan today.

Love of the sentence. Confining yourself to one of your choosing for the rest of your life, you select the jailer's remark to Socrates. I should want a page of Dostoevsky, Faulkner or Joyce, long convolutions crammed with qualifiers, rich with detours, disputations, prospects.

In Pech de L'Aze archeologists found the rib of an ox 300,000 years old, carved with festooned double arcs. Not a poem but symbolism. Even then, before Neanderthals, we craved/carved meaning. Even then a back was betrayal.

The worst part of being betrayed is feeling worthy of betrayal. It expunges poetry. One cannot even see the peaks where words nest in solitude and longing.

Inviting love on behalf of another, you must know the other, craft a poem to fit his lips. Reading it, must make the recipient feel she is kissing him after the walking-all-night-by-the-river date.

NEVER WHERE YOU ARE

1.

Morning with mist and Sonny Rollins,
oranges, a lazy walk – saxophone life.

Having swallowed the sky entire
the poet burped lovely clouds.

Each spring for days
snakes slather across the yard.

Under the crumbling foxholes of Europe
skeletons in tunnels.

Weaned on old music, she clasps
contagious words to her wounds.

Therapy of names by the sweet peas –
Trails of Tears, Princess Feathers, Patience.

2.

Pens have become keys
and still nothing opens easily.

Your heart safe in a box of leaves,
you wonder why your feet are cold.

The sea wants our penance for not
being sailors, wasting its mysteries.

Listen. The clouds break conclave.
A new sky has been chosen.

October. Geese once again in flight.
You incline south, I look north.

One always says more than intended;
one, less. Which are you?

The parrot in the bingo parlour
never once said bingo.

An abundance of excellence
mars the dance.

3.

From the feather of a hawk
you fabricate flight and strike.

On the sidewalk someone has drawn
a flying bird in green chalk.

The plank for a sinking friend
yanked from your lifeboat floor.

Lilacs last a day indoors.
Husband and wife shouting a storm.

Detours, delays, entanglements,
retreats– these are the only way.

I won't trust words she vows:
A windmill without wind.

I hold you in me the way
a forest holds wolves on a winter night.

Destinations are rivers.
You are never where you are.

Our brains conjure harmonies. These
lines will not stay isolate.

I Love(d) You

~

TURNING TO BRICK

I tell no one about you.
Even now. Here. These words
discreet as the old cigarette
ads painted on the sides
of crumbling buildings.
                                        Ladies
with long lashes turning
back to brick.

The ad's designer a big city
boy from somewhere
small who stayed small.

But weren't we something –
bright and slender as cigarette holders
pressed on scarlet lips?

We were our dreams incarnate.

If only we had known.

THE TRANSIT OF VENUS

Venus is rolling across the sun
on the TV screen above our heads.

Aglow, you speak of work,
your sister, a garden project.
You touch my hand, whisper,
Look, the waitress, how beautiful,
and I look and see she is lovely.

You place your hand on my arm.
and then speak of the one grief
that shadows your life.

I tell you what I have read:
No one alive has ever seen Venus
roll across the sun like this.
In 2012 she will do it again
then not for 105 years.
The passage takes under two hours.

We speak of the transit of Venus
and what makes beauty.
Is it our eyes, our dreams, the forms
we make to frame our griefs?
Whether it is the stepchild of time.

As our words move across my mind,
I see how beautiful we are.

BLUE BALLOON

The balloon with your breath in it
grows smaller each hour,
skin creasing a darker blue,
contracting in prophecy,

the way memory condenses
on slivers of evidence.
Before you left did we clasp
shoulders in our old half hug?

Death eases in by trifles.
I take the balloon in my hands,
on its wrinkled skin feel
for where your breath escapes.

Rituals of farewell conceal
the pain of departure. I recall
your lips on the blue globe,
cheeks puffed, face eclipsed

behind the growing sphere. Later,
as always, I said, *Drive carefully.*
In the stabbing aloneness after
you left I kissed the balloon

and as the skin pushed back
had premonitions of a wreck,
feared I held in my hands
all your breath left anywhere.

MARIONA

If half your face did not hold light
clear and clean and the other half
did not hide in shade, one eye
lustrous, the other mysterious;
if your nose were not elegant,
ending in a delicate indentation
of your lips, the upper one and thin,
the lower smaller, fuller; if your
chin did not appear slight and frail
and white against your black collar;
and if a wide band of black hair
did not fall straight over the corner
of your right eye and cheekbone,
merging with the darkness there,
and curve around the corner of your
mouth and curl beneath your chin,
and if at the same instant in the dim
light I hadn't looked up from my book
as you looked across the table, none
of what happened would have happened.

SEASONS OF YOU

1.

Amidst the copper pyrite blitz,
the pans of flash,
the ersatz rhinestones,
and bland razzmatazz
there's you, without antecedent,
moonlit.

I'm pulled through
the stethoscope of your attention
until there's just two of us
in the universe.

I confess I don't think of you
in one season more than the others.

Like radio signals from deep space
you pierce me constantly.

2.

Once on a teeming foreign street
a tall woman slipped from a doorway,
clasped my shoulders
looked hauntingly in my eyes
and walked into the crowd.
It was you.
                    It should have been you.
Strangers in a city not our own, mine
distant, yours nonexistent.
How could you make a home
on the rubble of your past?
Your mother eroded with care.
Your father ever at your door.
The hymns you sang jangled
in a bombed-out cathedral.

3.

Dazed in bright space, we wasted
our latent dreams,

signalled with whispers of smoke
from a snowy landscape,

our pale fires invisible beneath
the precaution of hills.

What we might have been is a whim
in the raging wind,

but it will not expire, lodges
in hedges of recollection.

We have no present, no future, live
in fraying memories.

Is it too late? It was always,
always too late.

I KEPT YOU

I kept you out of death
you unpolished monument,
askew, fissured, crumbling
into my heart.

So others could find you,
the part you made public,
suitably impressive
when they came with homage.

It took you a lifetime to die
as you intended, resisting
yet grateful for my arms
grateful at last for life.

You had to create so much
forgiveness from such spare
makings I stayed with you
though often I despaired.

Now I fumble attending
to myself, the awkwardness
of leisure, the awful bother
of being free of you.

THE ORACLE AT LEBADEA

I swayed out after a day in the cave
and you touched my bare arm,
your hand warm on my skin.

Walking hunched for hours
I had lurched into Trophonius' Throat
and collapsed on a limestone shelf.

Darkness crushed my torch,
the leaking stalactites,
the reek of a black pool.

A few hours shivering on the rock
and a voice from the gloom hissed
what might be expected – war,

famine, plague, nature strangled,
love strangled. Nightmares from the past
all well afoot. Still, I was quaking,

unwilling to leave. Hours later
what hauled me out was another
cave, a pit inside of me, full of

hunger, not just for the golden
loaves of local bread, something else,
an egg of light that wanted life.

When I emerged to your hand
the light exploded and outshone
the sunlight, it was so aroused.

MY FEAR OF TAKE OFF

The physics of flying I know:
the lift of the flat-based wedge with speed.
At 30,000 feet
it comforts me to think
aeronautical engineers
have calculated the drag
of every rivet on the fuselage,
the resistance of air
for all altitudes and headwinds
and their effect on fuel reserves,
that tables tell how far we can wobble
on just one engine in a storm.

All homage to our instructors:
the eagle and hawk,
the osprey and heron.

It's those other perils of flight
that leave me clutching
my personal flotation device.

The space between you and me –
What ratio of safety in spanning that?
How long could we fly before
drag exceeded thrust? And if we did
get off the ground, if we did soar over
resistance and defeat headwinds
with limitless mid-air refuelings,
how long before Control
talked us down or something
in our baggage exploded?

YOUR FEAR OF LANDING

I tell you it's a routine descent:
white-water clouds ridden
all the way down from the dizzy
zone. As we nose into a pool of
blue at an easy angle watching
the earth turn explicit
with forests, lakes, highways,
the sprawl of the city,
we no longer speak.

Homes full of love
compromised and disguised,
transmuted to prose.
And loveless homes
looking the same. We pretend
our separate vehicles
will not go to any of those.

As the craft throttles down
shrieking resistance
we turn from the window,
check each other's eyes, see
controlled doses of nothing.

When the wheels pound earth
we look straight ahead. We bounce
once, then the flaps screech against
our speed as we are held back
by one of the laws of physics.

DESIRE PACES

Desire paces alone outside your house
along the hedge where you used to hide.
It wants you out, in flight, your skin alive
the way water makes it alive everywhere
at once until you can't take another wave.
It wants to be inside your voracious flesh
under the moist warmth of a mouth you crave,
one worth all the goods you've traded for
this night. The serpent tongue that licks
until you turn numb with anticipation
for the glut rush prolonged even longer.
It wants you wanting more and getting it
in degrees so slow your brain seethes.
It wants the pale underskin of your arm
to glisten when it tongues along its length
to lick the soft nook inside your elbow.
It wants you to think there never was
nor will be anything so perfect as now.

BY WAY OF COINCIDENCE

Coincidence must seem but not be
planned, a conjunction of vectors
making amazement.

It will always happen to people
with mirrors, those who watch
reflections in windows.

Is it possible (and yes it is, even now,
even this late) that I am thinking of
you while you think of me?

No chance involved were we newly
smitten, our focus more constant
than pilgrim hands.

But given our map of estrangement,
such distances, such glaciated
mountains of time,

the real coincidence might be you
reading this and believing it is about
you, which it is.

RECORDERS

Cassius was right: the walls have ears.
And the floors and ceilings, rocks and trees,
their cells basins of conservation.

Technicians can replicate antiquity:
sandals on marble, the hacking of axes,
leather smacking flesh. All voices in all tongues:
great gouts of prating and gauzy collusions.

Each generation bleating.
The earth bleeding noise.

Most common: the banshee wind.
The pain of being voiceless so keen
it screams and some believe it is spirits
twisting the limbs of trees,
wheezing through parched wheat.

The lies you told me, my lies to you
vibrate somewhere in these walls
and, released, will reveal
we were never in love as we dreamed

NOTE SLIPPED BENEATH A CLOSED DOOR

1.

This music I hear now, piano filigree
over a surge of violins, you do not wish to hear
about. Nor the distress of your former
friend mired in despair. Nor the cancer
in remission in the lung of another.

I will certainly not intrude with the news
that just after five this morning, the sun
honeyed the southern hills with its version
of this same music and, for the occasion,
a squadron of cranes graced the sky.

2.

Silence always wins. It can mean
whatever we want: harmony unbroken,
nothing at all, a lethargy, a doubling-over
pain. Readings of wordless space are vain,
the white expanse of hopes unspoken.

After the end of everything, silence will
ascend without wings, to preside over
nothing, not even the combined
vacancies of all our emptinesses
pocked with the echoes of futile guesses.

    [steps to one side]
        the gray cat rubs
        your pant leg
            inconvenient fur,
            strange staccato purr
        static thoughts in your head
        needs to be nudged away
    [steps back]

No words.

This is pantomime
and simultaneous universal sign language
that has been transcribed for the page.

If you hear this
your brain is rephrasing motion.

Words would tremble, stumble, baffle
at the drop of a –

There is no blame. Today
betrayal is traded
for survival.

You knew it wouldn't continue

    not with irony dead and crated
    the words all desecrated
    the plague of drivel people crave
    and love on sale at the Ultrasave.

You knew
but I didn't, expected to
brood on until my doom,
hatching these things
with their miniature faces
yours/mine

or until . . .

oh well

oh

well

The Absent as if Present

~

NOTE TO THE ABSENT AS IF PRESENT

Mid-March, 4 a.m., fierce blizzard rampaging
and gnawing indoors, too, my hands and feet.
Winter holding on can mean I'm not dead.
Nor you and all the others we love to have
alive with us. Unlikely though we will ever
meet, you and I, each of us beleaguered
and euphoric at certain times, in certain
places, none the same, a special sort of
loneliness from someone never to be
present who might have been if only.
After a while here I will try once more
to sleep before the brusque demands of day.
It's been good to speak with you like this.
Thrive in love. And give the others mine.

K MATTER

We knew you were there concealed in darkness,
wearing black, the old conjurer's ruse.
We saw your influence on others, their
curious diversions and depressions,
the ways they became suddenly eccentric
as if they discerned others, spirits
invisible to us, here in the room.
And so we came to our belief in you.

Galaxies rotate between you and us
a few with suns and planets that may
have created more observers of space
who may have discovered you as well.
Mapping darkness is our common enterprise
before we pass into it ourselves.

ACKNOWLEDGEMENT

We've been together over fifty years,
turned into each other's clichés,
not even aware we compensate
for the other's deficiencies.
When I tire, you provide a yawn.
When I pine, you sigh.
I've grown to accept your losses,
your skin eruptions, your chronic
insomnia, your creaky hinges.
And you, old friend, no longer
ulcerate over my insecurities,
my routine mismanagement
of your essential regimens.

I appreciate that you
have all but stopped expecting
expensive lathers and lotions,
swank accessories and fashions,
daily walks, high-fibre snacks,
a ban on chocolate and beer,
that you now tolerate seeing
and hearing less and the strain
when the handles fall off
the names we used to heft with ease.

This accord is our triumph,
not to rile each other too much
before the certain sundering.

SYLVIA PLATH'S LAST RECORDING

Your voice is all I have.
At thirty, tense, throaty
from too much tobacco.
The longer vowels, exhaled
in cadence, shake.

At times a sour rasp,
syllables agitated
jutting over fingers
that clasp your throat.
Fierce complaints
against the universe
and that one deep pain –
your failed saviour-saints.

The hard bite of consonants,
a barbed-wire embrace for
inmate memories, midnight
visions, while down a flight
of clanging stairs, the girl,
twenty, chained, eyes shut,
feels voices crank the cables
tighter and tighter yet.

They placed you in a container
and they put it in the ground,
but you will not be restrained
this time will you? I confess
no one but you could kill you
with the requisite finesse,
the rhymed departure note.

So. So here we are: your voice
and I in this room alone
hanging used flesh back
on used bone, replacing
your shyness, your gracious
distress, your long fingers
straying again to your neck
like children playing.

And this poem, its own
hands to its throat, keen
for release, its eyes on you:
slim, long-waisted, down
a thin corridor of words,
your hand raised, waving –
but not to say goodbye.

WHAT GIVES THE SHINE TO EVERYTHING

Quarter past mid-life,
a child of light

and its medium,
a guide to its disguises.

It halos your hair,
scrimshaws your brow.

The page, light.
The pen, shadow.

Their juncture
your synthesis.

How else for us to see
unseen lines,

the ear's apparition,
the magpie heart?

COYOTE

for Andy Suknaski

1.

You always said you were dying
faster than Wood Mountain
                                        and you were

a forest fire on the plains
blazing from the inside out

furious to eat
the dryness of things

leaving blackness deeper   wider
than coulees

the smoke giving life to other lives
with images
          with words
                                    with omens

2.

The coyote surrounded/hounded
by too many weapons

hunted/haunted
snarls and in the hardened land

gouges a lair
none of us has yet to find

3.

You scrawled words
They were not enough

You drew pictures
Not enough

Pictograms
Not enough

Never is there enough of anything
good

4.

Wind-driven fires
in grasslands in bush

Herds rampage, stomp fences
Cities clog with smoke

Oh but the sunset last night
blistered with such beauty

I thought of you
Coyote
      holed up
                      no room for hope
                                                  riding it out

THAT ONE TALENT

for John Newlove

After you are lopsided by the stroke
that smears your words to mush and silences
your hands, the poems are stopped, as they say,
for good.
                    But it is not good to be fed
and watered, to be diapered as acts
of love or otherwise and not to have
release for that quickening tension.
It is not good to be full of poems,
the surge of them still mad in your blood,
and no pills to mute the call, to lie
awake at night and pray to trade this curse
for blindness.
                    Or not to fill with poems
yet believe they are wasting in your system
like the seeds of gods never to be praised.

A POET SO ADMIRED

for Mark Strand

A book on your lap, you sit
in a stuffed chair beneath
an elegant floor lamp, right half in
light, left in darkness –
your own symbol of polarity.

You are a poet so admired
other poets take notes when
you sneeze. They write poems
about your poems, speak
devoutly of your tropes.

You are a poet so envied
other poets dive from your line
breaks and delight in tales
of your carousing, even contrive
lies such as the one about how

you peed on a rubber plant
in the swanky lobby of
a deluxe hotel in Rome while
reciting a sonnet by Petrarch
in the original old Latin.

Tonight, a humid mid-July,
a single snowflake shivered
into your mind. It strayed
from the blizzard you placed
in a poem years ago.

You feared it might return
like this, having taken a life
of its own, on the prowl
for a final significance,
on the prowl for its maker.

INTERCESSIONS OF WEATHER

For two weeks there have been no stars
no sun
        just drizzles and peltings

You have been dying all this time
and not telling anyone
                                        You inquire why
I think you should

I never put it that way
asked only if you were content
to go alone

You tell me of your grandfather
walking his dog in winter
later in a blizzard
the dog returning alone

You say that would be good

You do not say *home*
or *friends*, or *love*, or *dead*

You do not say *hospital*
or *tubes* or *injections*
        spasms or *deliriums*

Rain smears the window behind
you
    Already
I am on the other side

NOT A MARRIAGE BUT

You persevered
In spite of our limitations
our distractions
our dissonance
you're still here

And if that's not a marriage
of true minds
it is a relationship
rare as mating
whooping cranes

The park was small
the walk brief
the talk the best
we could devise
given the impediments

Infinite space from
here to there   time
clogged with curiosities
all bridged by your gift
for unwinding mine

A FEW WORDS

after a line by Ruth Stone

A few words to let you know that last night
the moon was clouded dim but two close stars
jeweled off in the west like exotic eyes
and the fresh snow gleamed a fragile blue
with dark purple shadows among the heaves
of the far hills such that you wanted
a paint brush, and an owl wobbled on
the cold air trying hard not to be alone.
My footprints curving around the brink
of the pine woods were starkly black, like
letters winding down a page, a spiral line.
At the hill's crest I stopped and looked back
to read the scrawl: I love you, it said.
See what you miss by being dead?

Notes

~

"You, You, You or You" (p. 15): the quoted section is from the poem "You" by W. H. Auden.

"The Poem of the Act of the Mind" (p. 20): the title is from the last line of *Of Modern Poetry* by Wallace Stevens.

"Rejection Note" (p. 42): Marsyas is the centaur who acquired Athene's flutes after she abandoned them because she felt playing made her look uncomely. She considered this disrespectful and had him beaten. Persisting, he became so proficient he challenged Apollo, for which audacity Apollo had him flayed alive.

"To Sarah Who Wrote a Love Poem for a Friend" (p. 71): the poet in the title is Sarah Manguso.

"The Oracle at Lebadea" (p. 85): Trophonius, the oracle at Lebadea, was the opposite of the one at Delphi in that his woeful utterings cast people into gloom. Trophonius and his brother had constructed the temple at Delphi, but he had murdered his brother and for punishment was swallowed by the earth and became an oracle.

"By Way of Coincidence" (p. 89) is based on the article, "Just a Coincidence," by Stephen Osborne in *Utne Reader*, May-June 2003.

"What Gives the Shine to Everything" (p. 102) is a response to "Past the Middle of My Life," by Lorna Crozier (*Whetstone,* p. 39).

"A Poet So Admired" (p. 106) alludes to the poem, "A Piece of the Storm," by Mark Strand

"A Few Words" (p. 110) was inspired by Ruth Stone's line, "See what you miss by being dead" in her poem "Curtains."

Gary Hyland is an award-winning Saskatchewan teacher, writer, activist, consultant, and editor. He has published two chapbooks and five volumes of poetry, including *Just off Main* (Thistledown, 1982), *Street of Dreams* (Coteau, 1984), *After Atlantis* (Thistledown, 1991), *White Crane Spreads Wings* (Coteau, 1996), *The Work of Snow* (Thistledown, 2003), *Hands Reaching in Water* (Hagios, 2007), and *Love of Mirrors* (Coteau, 2008). As a poet, he has received numerous awards in Saskatchewan Writers Guild competitions, including major manuscript awards in 1991 and 1995, and the John V. Hicks Memorial Award in 2003. As a teacher, he has been a recipient of the Hilroy Fellowship for innovative teaching practices, the Marshall McLuhan Distinguished Teacher Award for contributions to the profession, and the Joe Duffy Memorial Award for excellence in teaching English. As a volunteer and activist, he has received awards from SaskCulture, the Saskatchewan Writers Guild, and the Saskatchewan Parks and Recreation Association. He has also been awarded the Saskatchewan Volunteer Medal. He lives in Moose Jaw, Saskatchewan, where he was born, and where he was named Lifetime Poet Laureate (with Robert Currie) in 1991 and Citizen of the Year in 1998 and 2006. In 2007 he was named one of the 100 most influential graduates of the University of Saskatchewan in the past century.